USBORNE UNDERSTANDING SCIENCE

ATOMS AND MOLECULES

Phil Roxbee Cox and Max Parsonage

Designed by **Stephen Wright**

Illustrated by
Andy Burton and **Kuo Kang Chen**

Portraits illustrated by **Kevin Lyles**

Additional designs by **John Russell**

Series editor: **Jane Chisholm**

Scientific consultant:
Nick Christou

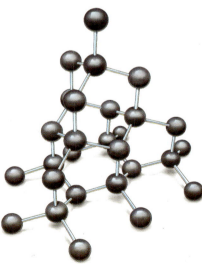

Contents

Words in *italic* type

Words which appear in *italic* type and are followed by a small star (for example: *conductor**) can be found in the glossary on page 31.

First published in 1992 by Usborne Publishing Ltd, 83-85 Saffron Hill, London EC1N 8RT, England.

Copyright © 1992 by Usborne Publishing Ltd.

The name Usborne and the device 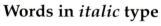 are Trade Marks of Usborne Publishing Ltd.

UE First published in America 1993.
    Printed in Spain.

Introducing atoms and molecules

The study of the tiny particles that are called atoms is a particularly exciting area of science because scientists are constantly finding out new and fascinating information. Atoms are really the basis of all science because most of the universe is made of matter, and all matter is made of atoms or parts of them. This book introduces you to the secret world of the atom.

There are different types of atoms, and these different types create different substances. But what makes one type of atom different from another? The answer lies in the atoms themselves. Each atom is made of even smaller particles. Although these particles are the same in every type of atom, their numbers vary.

A 15th century alchemist's laboratory

Despite a number of false claims, no alchemist ever succeeded in his task. Today scientists understand how, in theory, it would be possible to turn lead into gold. It could be done by altering the number of particles inside lead atoms. This would be a very complicated and expensive process, and would cause radiation.

The size of atoms

To say that atoms are tiny doesn't give the slightest hint as to how small they really are. The term 'microscopic' is given to something which is so small that it can only be seen under a microscope. Atoms are even smaller than microscopic. They cannot be seen under even the most powerful of ordinary microscopes.

To give you an idea of just how small atoms are, pour some salt into your hand. Now look at a single grain. This grain is made up of atoms. If each of these atoms grew to the size of the grain, the grain itself would be almost 10km (6.21 miles) across.

Pictures and diagrams

Throughout this book, there are many pictures and diagrams of the inside of atoms. It is important to realize that they are not drawn to scale. As you will find out, most of an atom is made up of empty space. If the distances between the particles that make up an atom were shown in relation to

the size of the particles, this book would be too big to fit on a shelf. In fact, it wouldn't fit inside a house.

Molecules

There are just over a hundred different types of atoms, and some types join with others to form molecules and compounds (see pages 14-15). If this did not happen, there would only be a hundred or so different substances in the universe. In fact there are millions. For example, an atom of oxygen can join up with two atoms of hydrogen to create a molecule of water.

Many types of molecule can, in turn, combine with other molecules to create yet more substances. So the more scientists understand about atoms and molecules, the more they begin to understand about everything around us.

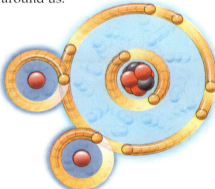
This water molecule is made up of two hydrogen and one oxygen atom.

Harnessing energy

Understanding the atom is one thing, but making use of that knowledge is another. In less than a century, scientists have learned how to harness some of the energy of the atom. Radiation and nuclear energy (see pages 24-25) come from atoms, and can be used both to help people and to destroy them.

With new ideas being put forward and tested all the time, there is still much more to be discovered and understood about the atom.

A butterfly and a flower are both made of atoms. What makes one a butterfly and the other a flower is the different numbers of particles inside the various atoms that combine to create them.

Altering atoms

The earliest chemists were called alchemists. They spent much of their time trying to change base metals (usually lead) into gold. Their work was a mixture of genuine experimentation and 'magic', and was usually shrouded in secrecy.

The growth of ideas

The idea that everything in the universe is made up of atoms is not a new one. There was a gap of over two thousand years, however, between people suggesting that atoms existed and scientists actually having the equipment and know-how to prove it. It was in Ancient Greece that the idea of the atom was born. The theory was a simple but radical one: that it could not be possible to keep cutting up something forever. There would come a stage where the particles would be so small that they could not be cut up any more. These particles are what we now call atoms, from the Greek word *atomos*, meaning 'uncuttable'.

Various views

The earliest record of this theory dates back to about 400 years BC, to two Greek philosophers called Leucippus and Democritus. They believed these uncuttable particles to be different shapes and sizes.

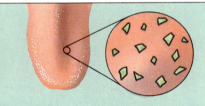

Some people believed that sour things were made of sharp particles that pricked the tongue.

Their ideas were discussed and taken up by a number of other Greek philosophers, including a man called Epicurus (342-270BC) who had great influence and a large following among Greek thinkers. The idea of the uncuttable particle was questioned by some philosophers, including Aristotle (384-322BC), perhaps the best-known of the Greek scholars.

Aristotle

Another early idea was that everything was made from earth, fire, air and water. These were called the four elements, and were thought to contain all the properties a substance could have: dryness, heat, cold and moisture.

Primary particles

The British chemist Robert Boyle (1627-1691) suggested that matter was made up of primary particles, some of which joined together to form larger particles called corpuscles. Today scientists would describe this as atoms bonding together to create *molecules**. It was Boyle who first used the word 'element' in its more modern form. He stated that elements were substances which could not be broken down chemically into simpler substances.

Dalton's theory

The British chemist John Dalton (1766-1844) first introduced the term 'atom' when he presented his Atomic Theory in 1807.

John Dalton

The main ideas of Dalton's Atomic Theory are:
- ★ All matter is made up of tiny particles (which he called atoms).
- ★ Atoms cannot be made, destroyed or divided.
- ★ Atoms of the same element are exactly alike.
- ★ Chemical reactions are the result of atoms rearranging themselves.
- ★ Atoms can join together to form larger particles in compounds.

Dalton later suggested that an atom could, after all, be split into even smaller particles, and was eventually proved right. Although he was wrong in thinking all the atoms of the same element were similar, his theory changed the face of science.

Most of an atom is made up of empty space between the particles.

This diagram of an atom is based on models by Bohr and Chadwick (see opposite). It shows electrons moving at high speed around a nucleus in the centre.

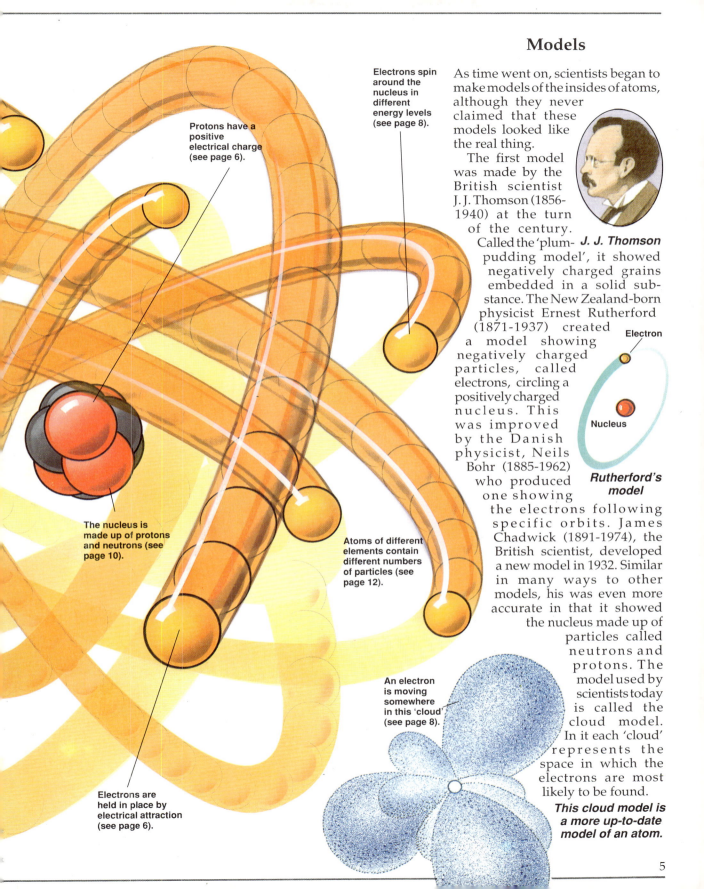

Models

Protons have a
positive
electrical charge
(see page 6).

Electrons spin
around the
nucleus in
different
energy levels
(see page 8).

As time went on, scientists began to make models of the insides of atoms, although they never claimed that these models looked like the real thing.

The first model was made by the British scientist J. J. Thomson (1856-1940) at the turn of the century.

J. J. Thomson

Called the 'plum-pudding model', it showed negatively charged grains embedded in a solid substance. The New Zealand-born physicist Ernest Rutherford (1871-1937) created a model showing negatively charged particles, called electrons, circling a positively charged nucleus. This was improved by the Danish physicist, Neils Bohr (1885-1962) who produced one showing

Electron

Nucleus

Rutherford's model

The nucleus is
made up of protons
and neutrons (see
page 10).

Atoms of different
elements contain
different numbers
of particles (see
page 12).

the electrons following specific orbits. James Chadwick (1891-1974), the British scientist, developed a new model in 1932. Similar in many ways to other models, his was even more accurate in that it showed the nucleus made up of particles called neutrons and protons. The model used by scientists today is called the cloud model. In it each 'cloud' represents the space in which the electrons are most likely to be found.

An electron
is moving
somewhere
in this 'cloud'
(see page 8).

Electrons are
held in place by
electrical attraction
(see page 6).

This cloud model is a more up-to-date model of an atom.

Inside the atom

Some atoms are only 1/100,000,000th of a cm (1/250,000,000th of an inch) thick. Others are larger, but it is still impossible to imagine their size (see page 3). Ten million atoms side-by-side would measure only 1cm (less than half an inch), which means that a single page of this book is nearly a million atoms thick.

At the end of the 19th century, scientists began to suspect that atoms themselves were made up of even smaller particles. As a result, revolutionary new theories were put forward which eventually led to amazing new discoveries. Each discovery was the result of scientific research, guesswork, luck and hundreds of hour of experimentation. Even today, scientists are finding out new and exciting things about what goes on inside the atom.

Subatomic particles

The particles inside atoms are called subatomic particles. In the middle of every atom is its nucleus. One useful way to think of the nucleus is as a sun at the centre of a tiny universe. This is how it appears in some of the early models (see pages 4-5). The nucleus itself consists of two types of subatomic particle: the proton and the neutron. A third type of subatomic particle spins around the nucleus. These spinning particles are called electrons. Electrons are by far the smallest of these subatomic particles. Their *mass** is only 1/1840th the mass of a proton.

Did you know...?

Most of an atom is made up of empty space. If it was possible to take the space out of all the atoms that make up the Empire State Building in New York, what remained would be smaller than a bag of sugar. Despite this, its mass would remain unchanged so that even the strongest crane could not lift it.

This is a more simplified diagram of an atom than the one on the previous page.

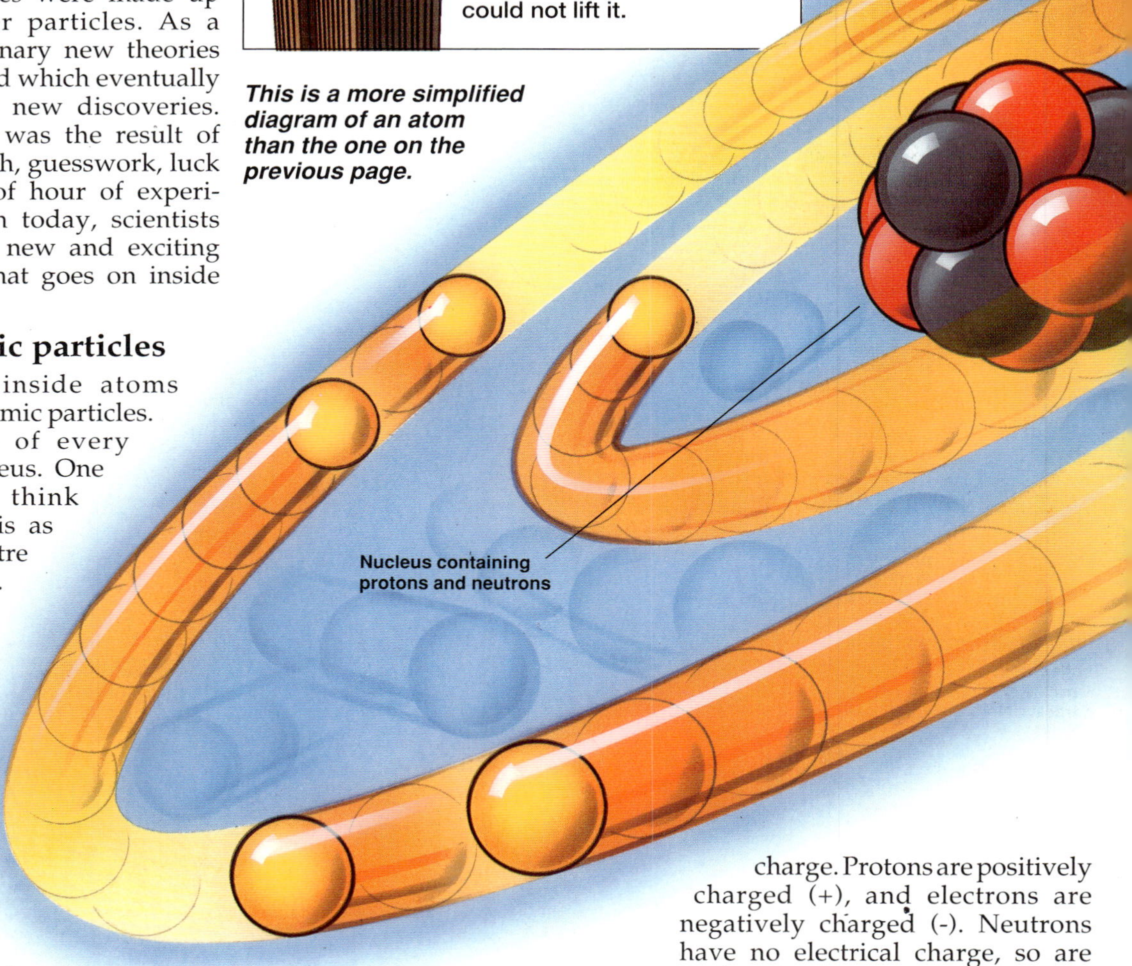

This diagram shows an electron spinning away from the nucleus. This doesn't actually happen because electrons are held in orbit by the protons.

Nucleus containing protons and neutrons

Electrical charges

Just how do a few tiny particles and some empty space hold together to make an atom? The answer has to do with electricity. Both protons and electrons have an electrical charge. Protons are positively charged (+), and electrons are negatively charged (-). Neutrons have no electrical charge, so are said to be neutral. Particles with opposite electrical charges are attracted to each other, in the same way that magnets with opposite poles stick together. It is the electrical charges that make the subatomic particles want to stay together.

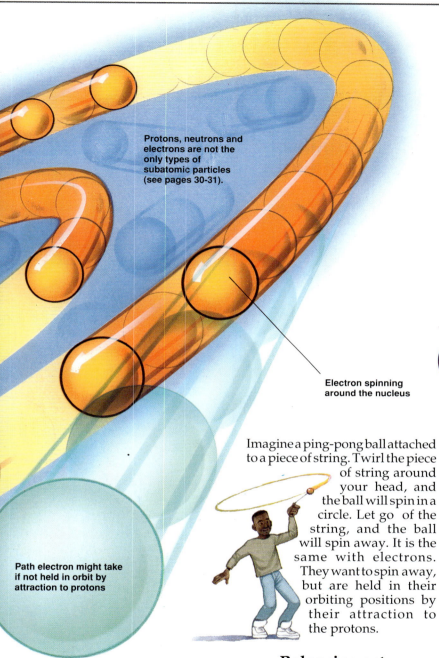

Protons, neutrons and electrons are not the only types of subatomic particles (see pages 30-31).

Electron spinning around the nucleus

Path electron might take if not held in orbit by attraction to protons

Discovering particles

Very few scientific discoveries are made in isolation. Each breakthrough comes after building on existing theories and experiments. This was the case with the discovery of subatomic particles. J. J. Thomson was just one of a number of scientists investigating atoms with a piece of equipment called a *cathode ray tube**. In the late 1890s he discovered electrons, which he called 'cathode rays'. Thomson went on to discover positively charged particles, which he called 'positive rays'. He built a cathode ray tube that showed cathode rays as a green glow and positive rays as a red glow.

A diagram of a cathode ray tube

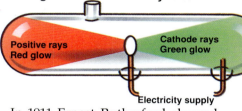

Positive rays
Red glow

Cathode rays
Green glow

Electricity supply

In 1911 Ernest Rutherford showed that an atom contained a nucleus, but it wasn't until 1932 that James Chadwick discovered the neutrons inside it (see page 5).

Imagine a ping-pong ball attached to a piece of string. Twirl the piece of string around your head, and the ball will spin in a circle. Let go of the string, and the ball will spin away. It is the same with electrons. They want to spin away, but are held in their orbiting positions by their attraction to the protons.

Balancing act

Even though protons are much larger than electrons, they both have exactly the same amount of electrical charge. Atoms have the same number of protons as electrons, so their electrical charges cancel each other out. This balancing act means that atoms are neutral and have no overall electrical charge. This is not the case with *ions**.

On the move

If electrical attraction keeps the subatomic particles together, why don't they form a large clump with no space in between? The reason is that the electrons are constantly moving. They never stop. This combination of attraction and movement lets the particles combine with the space to create an atom.

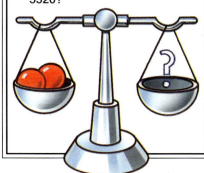

Quiz

★ Which is the smallest of these subatomic particles: a proton, neutron or electron?

★ Which has the greater electrical charge: a proton or an electron?

★ How many electrons would you need to equal the mass of two protons: 1840, 3680 or 5520?

The energy of electrons

Different electrons can contain different amounts of energy. The farther an electron is from the nucleus, the more energy it contains. Electrons with the same amount of energy are said to share the same energy level. They are each approximately the same distance from the nucleus. There are seven levels of energy in all.

Using this information, scientists can make a very basic model or diagram of an atom. Electrons with the same amount of energy are shown circling the nucleus at the same level, more commonly called a shell. These diagrams are really simplified maps showing the areas in which electrons of particular energy levels are most likely to be found. The edge of a shell is the boundary of one of these areas.

In theory, each shell can only hold a certain number of electrons before it is full. Scientists have worked out a set of rules which applies to most, but not all, atoms. One rule is that (starting from the first shell nearest to the nucleus) a shell has to contain its maximum number of electrons before any electrons can appear in any shells outside it. The number of shells and electrons in an atom affects the way it reacts with other atoms.

An atom with unfilled shells is more likely to be *reactive** than one with full shells.

Although a shell model is very useful for understanding the make-up and behaviour of an atom, it is important to remember that scientists do not claim that a real atom actually looks like this. Electrons cannot be pinpointed with such accuracy.

The modern electron cloud model shows electrons occupying blurred balloon-like areas called 'clouds'. Electrons with the highest energy levels occupy the largest clouds that stretch farthest from the nucleus.

An electron cloud model

Spaces show areas where electrons most likely to appear.

Nucleus

This model shows the rules governing the number of electrons in the first three shells. Beware: not all atoms follow these rules.

First shell, nearest nucleus, is full when it contains two electrons.

Second shell is full when it contains eight electrons.

When there are eight electrons in third shell (as shown), fourth shell can start to fill up.

Third shell can have up to eighteen electrons. Gaps show where extra electrons would go.

Real atom does not have hard outer-coating, unlike model.

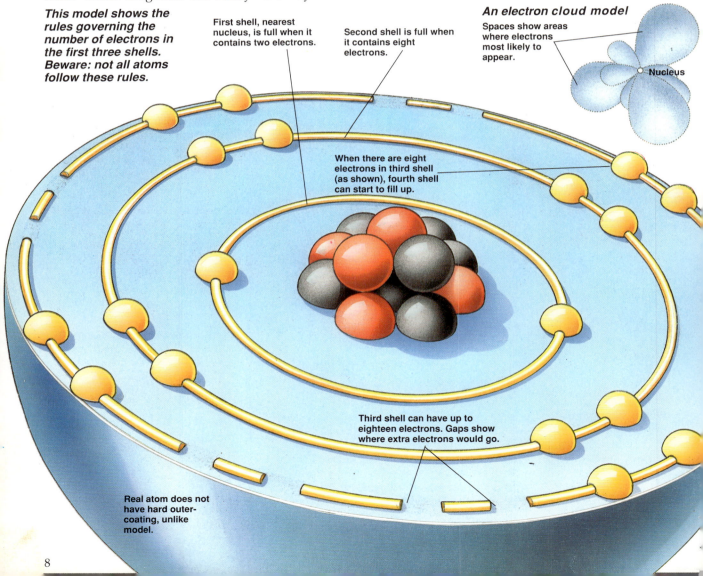

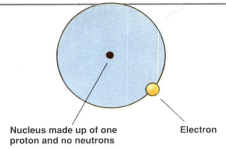

Nucleus made up of one proton and no neutrons

Electron

An atom of hydrogen (shown here) has only one shell, with only one electron in it. The shell is not full.

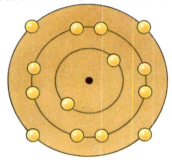

An atom of silicon (shown here) has three shells. Both of the inner shells are full, but the third (outer) shell has only four electrons.

Electrons in pairs

As you can see in the diagrams throughout this book, electrons often travel in pairs. All electrons are negatively charged, so why don't the electrons in these pairs repel each other? The reason is that they are spinning in opposite directions at the same time as they circle the nucleus. Although they share the same shell, one electron in the pair spins one way, while the other spins the other way. The paths that these electrons take are called orbitals. An orbital contains a maximum of two electrons.

The atom shown below has two electrons sharing an orbit. They each spin in opposite directions while moving around the nucleus.

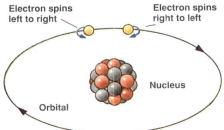

Electron spins left to right

Electron spins right to left

Nucleus

Orbital

Jumping electrons

The farther a shell is from the nucleus, the more energy its electrons possess. If electrons are exposed to heat or light, they can gain energy and become excited. They can then use this energy to jump from one shell to another which is farther from the nucleus. An excited electron may, for example, jump from the second to the fourth shell. It uses up most of its extra energy in the jump then falls back to its original shell. This is a bit like a ball being thrown up into the air, losing its energy, then falling back to earth with a thud. As it falls, the electron gives off the excess energy it has left in the form of *electromagnetic radiation** (often visible light). It is these falling electrons that make hot metals glow 'red hot'.

An electron being made to jump

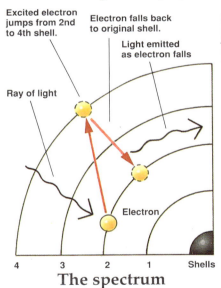

Excited electron jumps from 2nd to 4th shell.

Electron falls back to original shell.

Light emitted as electron falls

Ray of light

Electron

4   3   2   1   Shells

The spectrum

Scientists can deliberately excite the electrons of atoms into jumping. They can then measure the light the electrons give off when falling back to their original shells, using a machine called a spectrometer. The result can be photographed. The pattern of light produced by an atom and recorded in this way is called its line spectrum (plural: spectra). All atoms of the same element give off the same spectrum at the same temperature. Atoms of different elements have different spectra. In the same way that detectives can identify a person from his or her fingerprints, scientists can identify an element from its unique spectrum. Black and white or colour photographs of spectra can be used for this purpose.

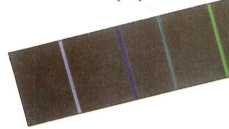

This is a part of the line spectrum of excited hydrogen atoms. It can be identified by the colour, spacing and position of the lines.

The sun's spectrum

In 1868 the British scientist Joseph Lockyer (1836-1920) studied the sun's spectrum. He identified certain elements but also noticed lines of light in positions unlike anything seen before. He thought that they indicated the presence of an unknown element, and called it helium, after *helios* the Greek word for the sun. Many people disagreed with him, claiming that it was a known element behaving strangely in the heat. Later helium was discovered on earth and Lockyer was proved to be correct.

The heart of the atom

In the heart of every atom is a nucleus, which is made up of neutral particles called neutrons and positively charged particles called protons. An atom is 10,000 times larger than its nucleus. If you wanted to draw a picture of an atom to scale, and you drew the nucleus the size of a pea, you'd have to make the atom bigger than a football stadium.

The role of the neutron

If there were no neutrons in the nucleus, scientists believe that an atom would fall apart. As the protons all have the same electrical charge, they want to push away from each other (because like charges repel). One of the neutron's roles is to keep the protons in place. The more protons there are in a nucleus, the stronger the electrical charge, and the more neutrons are needed to hold them together. Nuclei containing a relatively high number of neutrons, however, often break up, causing radiation (see page 24).

The nucleus of a phosphorus atom contains 15 protons and 16 neutrons.

The nucleus of a gold atom contains 79 protons, and 118 neutrons.

Atomic numbers

No two *elements** contain the same number of protons in their nuclei. The number of protons in an atom is called its atomic number. Simply by knowing an element's atomic number, it is possible to tell exactly what the element is. For example, an element made up of atoms containing six protons has the atomic number 6. This means it is carbon, as carbon is the only element with this atomic number.

Mass numbers

Atoms come in many sizes. The more protons and neutrons in an atom, the greater its *mass**. The number of protons and neutrons an atom contains is called its mass number. For example, one type of uranium is said to have a mass number of 238 because it contains 92 protons and 146 neutrons (92 + 146 = 238). Electrons are left out of the calculation because they add so little to the mass.

> ### Did you know...?
>
> A nucleus can decay if it becomes *unstable**. When this happens, a neutron can break up into a proton, an electron and even smaller particles. You can find out more about this on pages 24-25.
>
>

Elements and isotopes

Although a particular element is made up of one type of atom, these atoms often exist in a number of different forms called isotopes. The isotopes of an element all contain the same number of protons and electrons as each other. What makes them different is the number of neutrons. Some have more than others. This means that the isotopes of an element each have a different mass number, but all share the same atomic number. Most elements have isotopes. One isotope may be more unstable than another isotope of the same element. Unstable isotopes are *radioactive**.

If the different masses of all the isotopes of an element are added together and divided by the number of isotopes, you are left with the average mass of that element. This is called its relative atomic mass number (see page 20).

For example, carbon has three isotopes. The nucleus of a carbon atom is always made up of six protons, but each isotope contains a different number of neutrons. Scientists identify a particular isotope of an element by writing its mass number by its name.

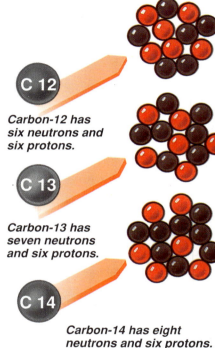

Carbon-12 has six neutrons and six protons.

Carbon-13 has seven neutrons and six protons.

Carbon-14 has eight neutrons and six protons.

Identifying atoms

The mass number of an atom helps to identify the element to which it belongs. (Some elements have the same mass number; for example, both calcium and argon have one of 40.) By knowing an atom's mass number, you are well on the way to identifying it.

Scientists can use a machine called a mass spectrometer to identify atoms. As the name suggests, the mass spectrometer uses the mass of the atoms as a part of this process.

Inside a mass spectrometer

Atoms are neutral, but if they are given an electrical charge they become *ions**. (This is explained in detail on page 15.) Inside the mass spectrometer atoms are turned into ions.

The ions of different elements and masses are then beamed through an electric field. This speeds up the ions in a process called acceleration.

The beam of accelerated ions then passes between two magnets, which create a magnetic field. Once inside the magnetic field, the path of the ions is bent. This is called deflection. The ions with the smaller mass are deflected more strongly than those with a greater mass. In this way, the machine divides up the ions in order of mass.

Now 'sorted' into relative masses, the ions are measured on a recording instrument. Sometimes this is a special photographic plate. Ions of the same type have the same mass, so they will hit the plate in the same spot. The photograph is then analysed.

By comparing the photograph with a standard chart, it is possible for scientists to calculate the mass of an ion from its position on the photographic plate. This then helps them to identify the different types of atoms. The machine is really measuring the mass of the nuclei, because electrons are too small to register.

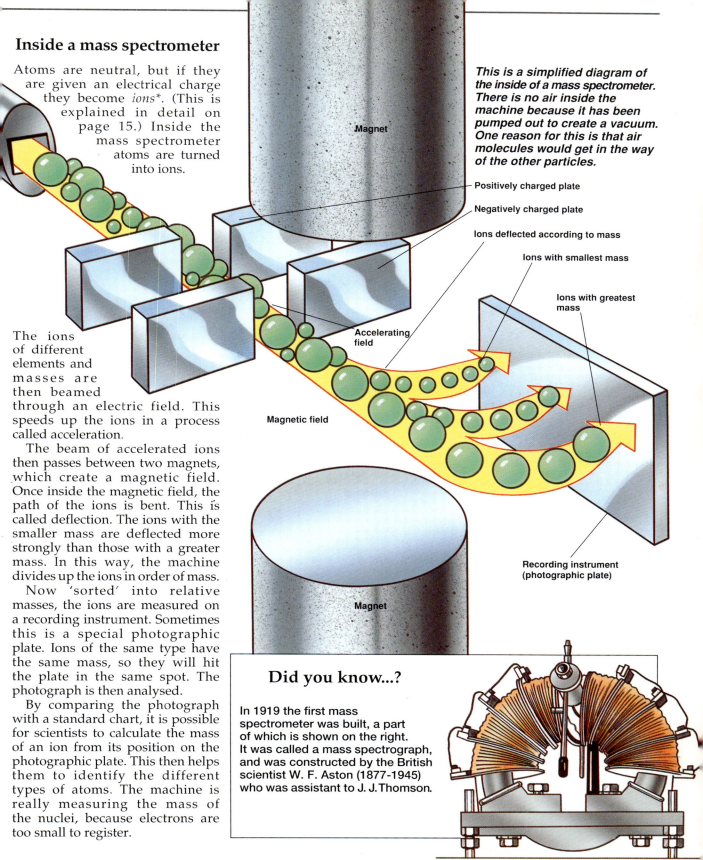

This is a simplified diagram of the inside of a mass spectrometer. There is no air inside the machine because it has been pumped out to create a vacuum. One reason for this is that air molecules would get in the way of the other particles.

Magnet

Positively charged plate

Negatively charged plate

Ions deflected according to mass

Ions with smallest mass

Ions with greatest mass

Accelerating field

Magnetic field

Magnet

Recording instrument (photographic plate)

Did you know...?

In 1919 the first mass spectrometer was built, a part of which is shown on the right. It was called a mass spectrograph, and was constructed by the British scientist W. F. Aston (1877-1945) who was assistant to J. J. Thomson.

Elements

Elements are the simplest substances there are, so it's impossible to break them down chemically into even simpler ones. This is because each element contains only one type of atom. For example, pure gold is an element. It contains gold atoms and nothing else.

Although there are only a hundred or so different elements, they can combine with each other to create every substance on the planet. About 90 elements occur naturally on Earth. The rest have been created by scientists.

Did you know...?

Scientists believe that more than 99% of the entire universe is made up of two elements: hydrogen and helium. They have calculated that, for every 10,000 atoms of hydrogen, there are 500 atoms of helium and only one atom of any other element.

Allotropes

The atoms of some elements, such as oxygen, sulphur and carbon, exist in a number of different forms called allotropes. Each allotrope of an element contains the same type of atom, but the atoms are arranged in a different order. This gives the substance a different structure, which affects its *physical properties** (such as strength and hardness). This means that different allotropes of the same element can look and feel very different. For example, diamond and graphite are both allotropes of carbon, but they are very unlike each other. They both contain only carbon atoms, but the atoms are arranged to form very different structures.

Graphite and diamond

Graphite is very common and has many uses, including lubricating engines, and as lead in pencils. In graphite, each atom is linked to three other atoms, and makes up a

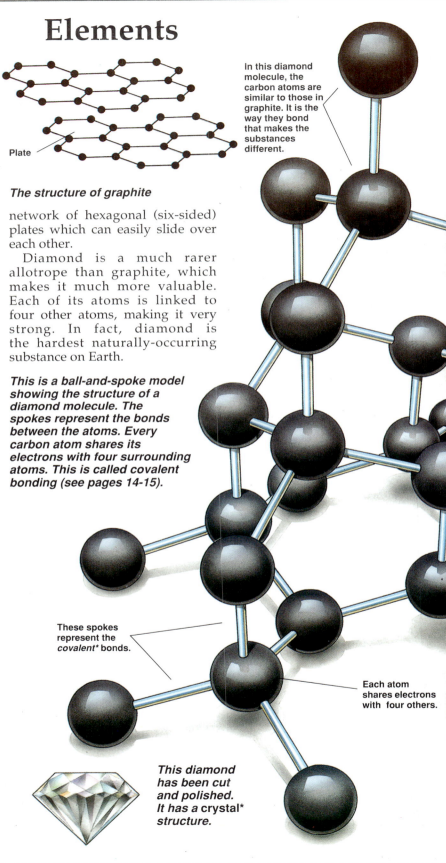

Plate

The structure of graphite

network of hexagonal (six-sided) plates which can easily slide over each other.

Diamond is a much rarer allotrope than graphite, which makes it much more valuable. Each of its atoms is linked to four other atoms, making it very strong. In fact, diamond is the hardest naturally-occurring substance on Earth.

This is a ball-and-spoke model showing the structure of a diamond molecule. The spokes represent the bonds between the atoms. Every carbon atom shares its electrons with four surrounding atoms. This is called covalent bonding (see pages 14-15).

In this diamond molecule, the carbon atoms are similar to those in graphite. It is the way they bond that makes the substances different.

These spokes represent the *covalent** bonds.

Each atom shares electrons with four others.

This diamond has been cut and polished. It has a **crystal** structure.

Types of elements

Elements are grouped according to their physical and chemical characteristics. There are three types of elements: metals, non metals and metalloids. Metalloids are sometimes grouped with non metals, but they can be made to act like either.

Metals

Well over half of all elements are metals. All metals are solid at room temperature, except for mercury. Metals are good *conductors**, which means that electricity and heat flow easily through them. Metals that are flexible enough to be bent without snapping are said to be malleable. Some malleable metals are used to make electrical wires. All metals are shiny when cut, and a few are magnetic.

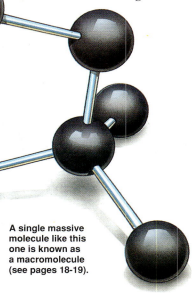

A single massive molecule like this one is known as a macromolecule (see pages 18-19).

Native metals and ores

Although most elements are metals, only four metals - gold, silver, platinum and copper - can be found naturally as pure elements on earth. They are known as the native, or 'noble', metals. All other metals are found in compounds called ores, from which the pure elements must be taken out.

Lead ore can be found as crystals in limestone rock.

Metal alloys

Many of the metals people use are not pure metal elements. They are a mixture of different metals and some non metals. These mixtures are called alloys. Brass is an alloy of copper and zinc. Copper is used to form many common alloys, including cupronickel (copper and nickel). Most silver-coloured coins are made from cupronickel.

Cupronickel coins

The most common metal is iron. In its pure form its uses are limited, because it is brittle and can break easily. By mixing it with carbon and other elements, however, the alloy steel can be created. Steel is much stronger and more flexible than iron. Surprisingly, as little as 0.2% carbon mixed with iron can create steel strong enough to build bridges which carry heavy traffic.

Non metals

There are only sixteen non metallic elements. At ordinary temperatures, four of them are solids, one is liquid, and the other eleven are gases. All non metals, except graphite, are poor conductors of electricity and heat.

Most of the commonly used non metals are gases. Helium is a gas which is lighter than air. It is used to fill modern airships to make them float in the sky. Earlier airships used hydrogen, but this was very dangerous because hydrogen burns in air.

The Hindenburg **was an airship filled with hydrogen. On 6th May 1937, the engines caught fire, setting alight to the hydrogen. The airship burst into flames and 36 people were killed.**

Metalloids

Metalloids are the elements which are neither metal nor non metal, but can be made to act like one or the other. There are only seven metalloids, and they are all solids. Depending on how they are treated, they can be made to conduct electricity like metals, or act as poor conductors (known as *insulators**) like non metals.

This tiny microchip is made from the metalloid silicon.

Mixtures and compounds

If you ate some sodium or breathed in some chlorine you could die, but you've eaten the substance they combine to make: sodium chloride. It's just common salt. But why are the combined elements safe, when the individual elements are not? The answer is that the new substance is the result of a chemical reaction, which gives it different properties from the substances it's made from. New substances formed as a result of a chemical reaction are called compounds.

Most things on earth are made up of more than one element. They are described as being either compounds or mixtures. Unlike compounds, mixtures are simply different substances (elements or compounds) mixed together without a chemical reaction occurring. Most mixtures keep the same properties as their original ingredients.

Creating mixtures

Mixtures make up most natural forms of matter on earth, and many man-made substances too. The proportions of the different ingredients in a mixture can vary. For example, a mixture of salt and pepper can contain as much salt and as much pepper as you choose. The ingredients of mixtures can be separated without a chemical reaction, as they are held together by physical rather than chemical means.

Making compounds

Unlike mixtures, compounds contain elements combined in a fixed proportion. This proportion of ingredients cannot vary. There are two types of compounds: covalent and ionic.

Covalent compounds

Covalent compounds are created by atoms of different elements sharing electrons. Usually non metals do this with other non metals. The sharing of the electrons bonds the atoms together to form new molecules. Water is an example of a covalent compound.

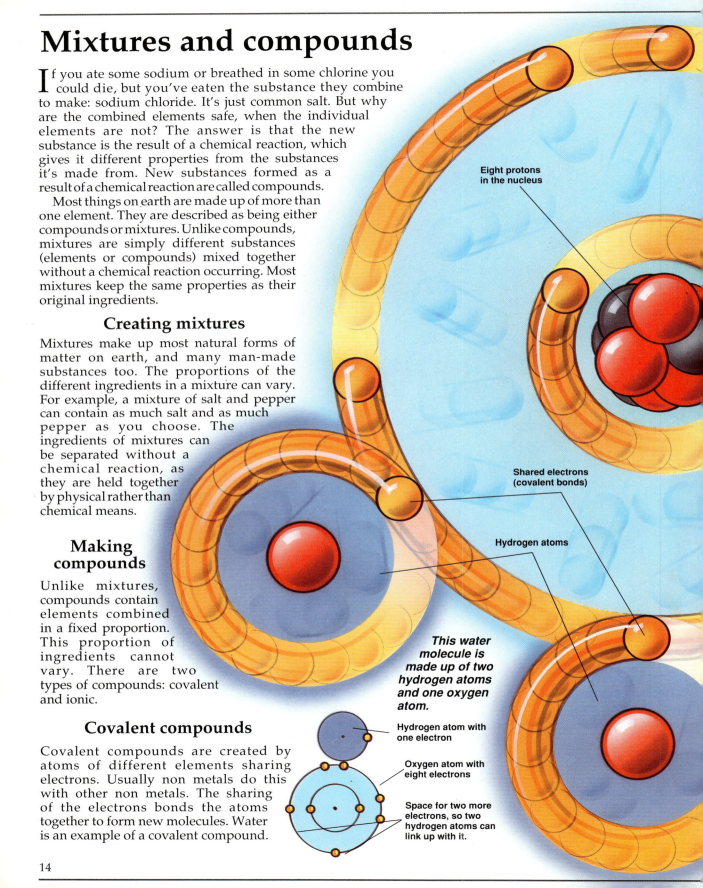

Eight protons in the nucleus

Shared electrons (covalent bonds)

Hydrogen atoms

This water molecule is made up of two hydrogen atoms and one oxygen atom.

Hydrogen atom with one electron

Oxygen atom with eight electrons

Space for two more electrons, so two hydrogen atoms can link up with it.

Oxygen atom

Ionic compounds

An ionic compound is formed when a metal atom loses an electron to a non metal atom. The metal atom becomes a cation and the non metal becomes an anion. The two are held together by the attraction of their opposite charges (see page 6) to form an ionic compound. Sodium chloride (common salt), which was mentioned earlier, is an example of an ionic compound.

A sodium atom contains 11 protons and 11 electrons, so it is neutral.

A chlorine atom also has no charge It has 17 protons and 17 electrons.

When the neutral sodium atoms react with the neutral chlorine atoms, each sodium atom loses an electron. These are gained by the chlorine atoms. This results in the formation of sodium cations and chlorine anions. Their opposite electrical charges attract them to each other, creating sodium chloride.

Sodium chloride

Molecular models

When studying compounds, scientists often use models. A model does not actually look like a real molecule, but it is a simple and useful way of showing the number of atoms that make up a molecule. There are two basic types of model: ball-and-spoke and space-filling models.

You can buy space-filling models like this one from specialist shops.

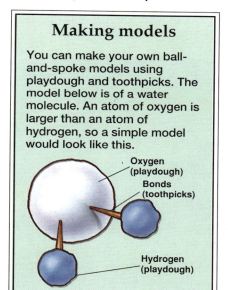

Making models

You can make your own ball-and-spoke models using playdough and toothpicks. The model below is of a water molecule. An atom of oxygen is larger than an atom of hydrogen, so a simple model would look like this.

Oxygen (playdough)

Bonds (toothpicks)

Hydrogen (playdough)

Symbols and formulas

All elements have been given a symbol of one or two letters. The first letter is always a capital, the second is always small. (For example sodium's symbol is Na.) When elements combine to form compounds, the symbols are joined to create a formula. For example, H is the symbol for hydrogen and O is the symbol for oxygen. When two atoms of hydrogen combine with one atom of oxygen to create water, the formula is written as H_2O. The number $_2$ means that two hydrogen atoms have joined with one oxygen atom. The symbols of most elements are shown on pages 20-21.

Ions

Certain atoms may gain or lose electrons. If an atom gains electrons, it will contain more negatively charged particles than positively charged ones. This gives the atom a negative charge. If an atom loses electrons, it will become positively charged. Electrically charged atoms are called ions. Positively charged ions are called cations. Negatively charged ions are called anions.

Reactivity

Some elements can gain or lose the electrons used for bonding more easily than others. These elements are said to be more reactive. Scientists have made a list of elements placing them in order of their reactivity. This is called the reactivity series. The more reactive the element, the more easily it will combine with other elements to form compounds.

Moving molecules

Billions of molecules in the air around you are hitting each other billions of times a second. They travel at speeds of over 1000 metres (about 1000 yards) per second. That's as fast as a bullet fired from a gun. They never actually travel 1000 metres at that speed because they keep crashing into each other. It is not just the molecules in air that are moving. All molecules vibrate, including the ones that make up this book.

Kinetic Theory

The idea that all matter is made up of moving molecules is called the Kinetic Theory, after the Greek word *kineo* meaning 'I move'.

The Kinetic Theory states:
★ All matter is made up of tiny moving particles.
★ Particles of different substances have different sizes.
★ Particles move faster as they get hotter.
★ Lighter particles move faster than heavier ones (at the same temperature).
★ In a solid the particles are close together and vibrate in fixed positions.
★ In a liquid they are farther apart, have more energy, and can move around each other.
★ In gases the particles are far apart and move rapidly and randomly to fill all the space they can find.

Brownian Motion

In 1827 the British biologist Robert Brown (1773-1858) first noticed the movement of tiny dust particles in liquids and gases.

Path of smoke particle can easily be seen under a microscope

He saw that they moved randomly (in no set pattern). What he didn't know was why they were moving. He thought that they were alive.

It wasn't until the 20th century that the German-born scientist Albert Einstein (1879-1955) worked out the reason behind what Brown had seen. He explained that the movement of particles, such as dust, is caused by them being hit by 'invisible' molecules that make up air. This movement of particles in liquids and gases is named after Brown and is known as Brownian Motion.

States of matter

Solids, liquids and gases are all different states of matter. Matter does not always have to stay in the same state. The state of the molecules that make up a substance can be affected by temperature. For example, some of the water in the saucepan below has turned to steam. The liquid has become a gas. When frozen, water becomes ice, a solid.

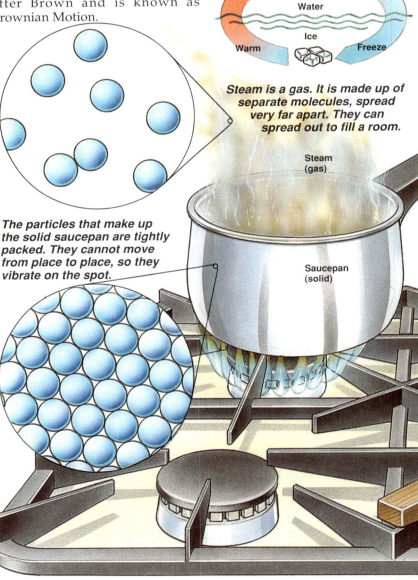

Steam
Heat   Cool
Water
Ice
Warm   Freeze

Steam is a gas. It is made up of separate molecules, spread very far apart. They can spread out to fill a room.

Steam (gas)

The particles that make up the solid saucepan are tightly packed. They cannot move from place to place, so they vibrate on the spot.

Saucepan (solid)

Heat and reactions

There are two kinds of reactions between substances: physical changes, such as changes of state, and chemical reactions, which involve the creation of a new substance or substances (see page 14). Both types of reaction are speeded up by heat. This can be seen by taking two glasses, one containing cold water and the other warm water. Drop a spoonful of salt into each glass at the same time and watch. In both cases the salt will dissolve, because the particles of salt break up and mix with the molecules of water. However, the warm water will dissolve the salt much faster than the cold.

Water is made of molecules that are touching, but can slide over each other, fitting any shape. They are easily pushed apart, which is why you can stir the water with a spoon.

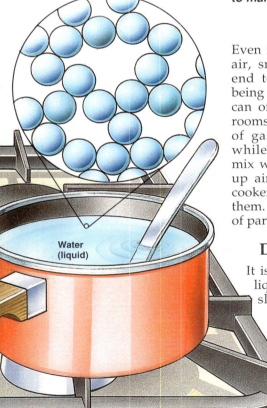

Water (liquid)

Friction

You can create heat by rubbing your hands together. The faster you rub them, the hotter they become. If you rub them too hard, they can hurt. As the molecules of skin are rubbed together, they knock into each other and move faster. Molecules of solids are prevented from sliding over each other by a force called friction. Fires can be started making use of friction. For example, rubbing a stick in a hole in a piece of wood packed with dry leaves can produce enough heat to start a flame. In some parts of the world, this method is still used to light fires.

Friction caused by stick rubbing in hole

An African fire-drill can be used to make a flame.

Diffusion

Even in a room without a flow of air, smells still spread from one end to the other. When food is being cooked in the kitchen, you can often smell the food in other rooms. This is because molecules of gas are freed from the food while it is being cooked. They mix with the molecules that make up air and move away from the cooker to fill the space available to them. The mixing and movement of particles is called diffusion.

Diffusion of liquids

It is not only gases that diffuse, liquids can too but usually more slowly. This is because the molecules of a liquid are closer together than those of a gas, so they take longer to fill the available space. For example, a drop of ink in a jar of still water takes time to diffuse and colour the water.

A colour race

This experiment shows diffusion in liquids, using a method called chromatography. You will need some bottles of food colouring and some coffee filters or blotting paper.

If you don't have any food colouring, you can get it from some brightly coloured sweets. Choose four sweets of different colours, and put each one in a separate saucer with very little water. In minutes the colour will be released into the water, leaving you with the liquid colouring.

Draw a pencil line 3cm (just over one inch) from the bottom of your paper.

Water   Sweet

Put a drop of colouring on the pencil line. Dry it, put a drop of the same colouring on top and dry it, and so on, until the colour is bright. Repeat this with the other colourings.

Roll the paper into a cylinder, keeping it in place with a paper clip. Now dip the bottom of the cylinder into a bowl containing 2½cm (1 inch) of water. Slowly the water will move up the paper, and the colours will diffuse, moving at different speeds through the weave of the paper.

Some of the colours will move farther than others. This is because they have different sized particles. Similar colours should move a similar distance. The particles with the least weight should move farthest*.

*A colour's journey can also be affected by how much its particles stick to the paper.

Massive molecules

Atoms sometimes link together to form massive molecules called macromolecules. (*Macro* is Greek for 'massive'.) Although bonds between atoms can be very strong, some macromolecules are weak in places because not all their atoms are linked to each other. Parts of their *structures** are held together by weak attractions. Materials made up of macromolecules include plastics, ceramics, glass and man-made fibres.

Plastics

Polythene, perspex and *PVC** are just three examples of plastics. All plastics are man-made, and are created using a process called polymerization. Polymerization is the linking together of small molecules, called monomers, to form long chains. These chains may, in turn, link up with other chains to create even more massive molecules. Molecules formed by the linking of monomers are called polymers, from the Greek for 'many bits'.

Monomers

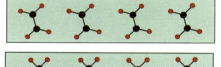

Monomers linked together to form a polymer

A useful thing about plastics is that, by mixing the different monomers, it is possible to design a plastic for a specific use. Some types of plastics soften when heated because they have unlinked polymers. These are called thermoplastics. Other plastics will not melt, because their chains of molecules are joined to each other. These are thermosetting plastics.

A thermoplastic, with unlinked polymers

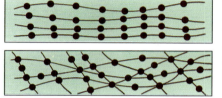

A thermosetting plastic, with linked polymers

Polythene and PVC are two polymers with very different properties. Whereas polythene is ideal for such things as foodwrap, PVC is stronger and can be used for luggage and clothing. New plastics can be created by heating and mixing together the monomers of existing polymers.

Ceramics

Ceramics are joined together in a similar way to polymers, except that each molecule is a crystal. The molecules are held together with covalent bonds (see page 14). Crystals have definite structures, and many have definite geometric shapes, straight edges and flat surfaces.

Nearly all man-made ceramics are made of clay (which is composed of tiny crystals of silicon dioxide and aluminium oxide) and a few other elements such as sodium, calcium and magnesium. Baked clay is used for pottery. The clay is shaped while it is still a soft mud, then baked in a

The diagram below shows a silicon dioxide crystal. Silicon dioxide is an ingredient of clay which, in turn, is the basis of most ceramics. Silicon dioxide is made up of silicon and oxygen atoms.

Silicon atoms are shown in red. They are surrounded by three oxygen atoms underneath and one on top.

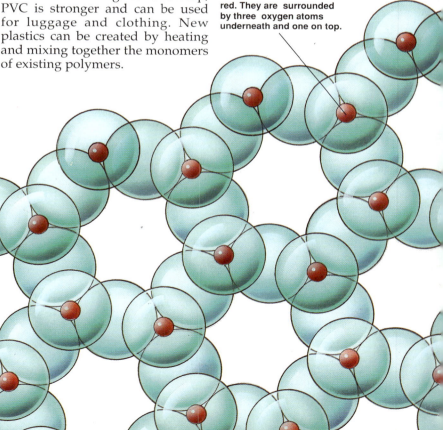

kiln. The baking makes the crystals link together to form a hard ceramic.

Natural ceramics include rock-forming crystals which have crystalized out of liquid lava. Some, found in slate, are created from clay under high pressure and temperature. They have been 'baked' by nature.

The edges of a ceramic's crystals are the weakest part of its make up. In much the same way that a small tear in a cotton sheet can soon become a big hole, a small crack in a ceramic can soon spread.

If a ceramic bowl cracks, the crack follows the edges of some of the ceramic's crystals.

Although ceramics are *insulators**, scientists have been developing new types which are highly efficient *conductors**. These new ceramics are called high temperature super-conductors, and are made of compounds not usually found in clay. Not only is this an amazing achievement, but it also means that in the future it should be possible to use these special ceramics to make items such as electrical equipment.

Did you know...?

NASA (the National Aeronautics & Space Administration) created a new type of ceramic tile, with special properties, to cover the outside of their space shuttles.

When re-entering the earth's atmosphere, the outside of a shuttle gets extremely hot. If the shell of the shuttle conducted the heat through it, the inside would be too hot for the astronauts to survive. The special tiles are made from the ceramic pyrographite. (*Pyro* is the Greek word for fire.) Rather than conducting heat through it, pyrographite conducts heat sideways. This means that the heat simply moves across the tiles and is dispersed, instead of going through the tiles and shell of the spacecraft.

Pyrographite tiles on a NASA space shuttle

Glass

Believe it or not, glass is a liquid. Like other liquids, it flows, but very slowly. This is why glass which is hundreds of years old is thicker at the bottom than at the top. Over time, it has flowed downwards.

Glass is not made up of crystals. The atoms in its macromolecules have no regular links, so it is not very strong.

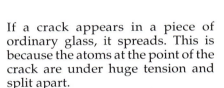
This long chain of atoms is linked together as one macromolecule of glass. Its molecules have no regular order.

If a crack appears in a piece of ordinary glass, it spreads. This is because the atoms at the point of the crack are under huge tension and split apart.

Most glass is man-made, mainly from sand and limestone, but glass can also be formed by volcanoes. This naturally-formed glass is called obsidian.

Man-made fibres

Nylon is probably one of the most common man-made fibres. It is used to make all types of clothes from suits to stockings. Nylon was created in the 1930's by scientists working under Wallace H. Carothers (1896-1937) for the Du Pont Company. Carothers and his team had experimented with many polymers, but what made nylon special was that it could be pulled out into thin strands. These strands can be used as thread to make clothes.

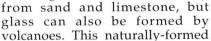
The process of pulling nylon into strands is called cold-drawing.

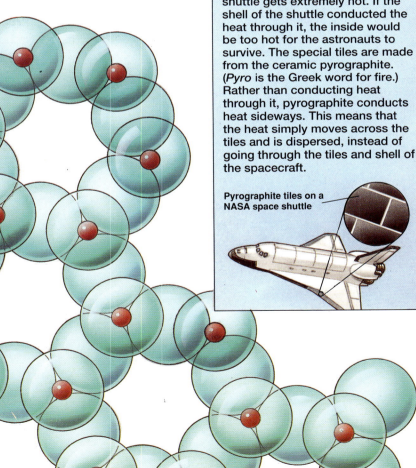

The periodic table

The modern periodic table is a table showing known *elements**, their symbols, *atomic numbers** and relative atomic masses. The position of an element in the table shows whether it is a metal, non metal, or metalloid. It also indicates what properties it possesses. The table got its name from the frequent, or periodic, repeating of the properties of similar elements. Today the table is taken for granted, but how did scientists first work it out? Throughout the 19th century, many scientists tried to create charts listing elements in order of the 'size' of their atoms. The idea was to try to find and show a relationship between the size of an atom and its properties, and to show a pattern of similarities between elements of a similar size. The size of an atom really means its *mass**. It is possible to calculate the mass of an atom in relation to other atoms, using the mass of Carbon-12 as a base. This is called relative atomic mass. (Relative atomic mass is sometimes referred to as RAM.) The relative atomic mass number of an element is the average of the masses of its *isotopes**. One way to imagine this is as an average mass of a sample of atoms in a particular element. The RAM of one particular element is always the same.

Early attempts

An early attempt to find a pattern in the properties of elements was made by the German chemist Johann Wolfgang Döbereiner (1780-1849). He noticed that some elements could be arranged in groups of three. An element in a particular group had similar properties to the other two elements in that group. As there were three elements to a group, Döbereiner gave them the name of 'triads' (which means 'groups of three'). He also discovered that if he put the elements of a triad in order of RAM, the

Döbereiner

RAM of the element in the middle was very close to the average RAM of the other two elements. Later, the English scientist John Newlands (1837-1898) arranged elements in groups of eight, but 'Newland's octaves', as they were called, were largely ignored by scientists.

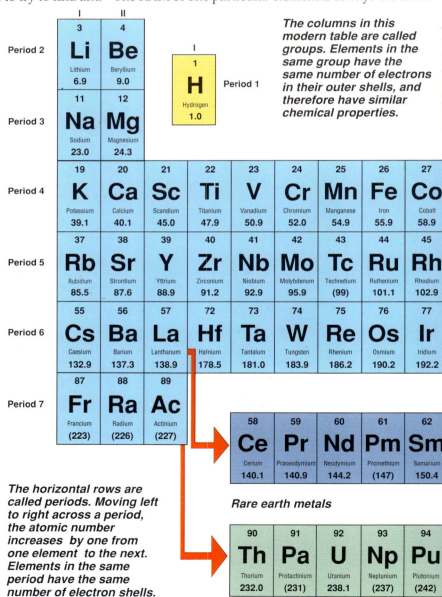

The columns in this modern table are called groups. Elements in the same group have the same number of electrons in their outer shells, and therefore have similar chemical properties.

Rare earth metals

The horizontal rows are called periods. Moving left to right across a period, the atomic number increases by one from one element to the next. Elements in the same period have the same number of electron shells.

Puzzle

Li Lithium RAM 6.9	Using the Döbereiner triad (left), try to work out the approximate relative atomic mass of sodium.
Na Sodium RAM ?	
K Potassium RAM 39.1	

Groups are numbered with Roman numerals, and some have been given names.

Number	Name
I	Alkali metals
II	Alkaline-earth metals
VII	Halogens
VIII (or 0)	Noble gases

Key:

Atomic number	50
Symbol	**Sn**
Name	Tin
RAM	118.7

Colour key:

- Metals
- Non metals
- Metalloids

Period 1

	VIII
	2
	He
	Helium
	4.0

III	IV	V	VI	VII	
5	6	7	8	9	10
B	**C**	**N**	**O**	**F**	**Ne**
Boron	Carbon	Nitrogen	Oxygen	Fluorine	Neon
10.8	12.0	14.0	16.0	19.0	20.2
13	14	15	16	17	18
Al	**Si**	**P**	**S**	**Cl**	**Ar**
Aluminium	Silicon	Phosphorus	Sulphur	Chlorine	Argon
27.0	28.1	31.0	32.1	35.5	39.9

			III	IV	V	VI	VII	
28	29	30	31	32	33	34	35	36
Ni	**Cu**	**Zn**	**Ga**	**Ge**	**As**	**Se**	**Br**	**Kr**
Nickel	Copper	Zinc	Gallium	Germanium	Arsenic	Selenium	Bromine	Krypton
58.7	63.5	65.4	69.7	72.6	74.9	79.0	79.9	83.8
46	47	48	49	50	51	52	53	54
Pd	**Ag**	**Cd**	**In**	**Sn**	**Sb**	**Te**	**I**	**Xe**
Palladium	Silver	Cadmium	Indium	Tin	Antimony	Tellurium	Iodine	Xenon
106.4	107.9	112.4	114.8	118.7	121.8	127.6	126.9	131.3
78	79	80	81	82	83	84	85	86
Pt	**Au**	**Hg**	**Tl**	**Pb**	**Bi**	**Po**	**At**	**Rn**
Platinum	Gold	Mercury	Thallium	Lead	Bismuth	Polonium	Astatine	Radon
195.1	197.0	200.6	204.4	207.2	209.0	(210)	(210)	(222)

63	64	65	66	67	68	69	70	71
Eu	**Gd**	**Tb**	**Dy**	**Ho**	**Er**	**Tm**	**Yb**	**Lu**
Europium	Gadolinium	Terbium	Dysprosium	Holmium	Erbium	Thulium	Ytterbium	Lutetium
152.0	157.3	158.9	162.5	164.9	167.3	168.9	163.0	175.0

95	96	97	98	99	100	101	102	103
Am	**Cm**	**Bk**	**Cf**	**Es**	**Fm**	**Md**	**No**	**Lr**
Americium	Curium	Berkelium	Californium	Einsteinium	Fermium	Mendelevium	Nobelium	Lawrencium
(243)	(247)	(245)	(251)	(254)	(253)	(256)	(254)	(257)

Dmitri Mendeleev

The modern periodic table owes its existence to the Russian scientist Dmitri Mendeleev (1834-1907). He collected all the information he had about each element on separate cards. He then sorted the cards into order of increasing atomic mass, and laid them out in a horizontal row. When he came to an element with properties similar to one he had already laid down, he started a new row directly beneath the last. This meant that elements in the same vertical column had similar properties to each other.

Mendeleev

Mendeleev found that there was a repetition of properties every eight or eighteen elements. When this didn't occur, he realized that there were probably some undiscovered elements. He solved this by leaving gaps, and by predicting what the properties of these missing elements would be. He was also confident enough to swap around a few elements when their mass did not match the patterns he had discovered. Mendeleev published the table in 1869. Scientists later discovered several new elements as a direct result of trying to fill in the gaps that he had left. The *properties** of these elements were startlingly similar to those Mendeleev had predicted. His table was accepted as a very important guide to the properties of elements.

The modern periodic table

The major fault in Mendeleev's table was that he believed that it was the mass of the elements that affected their properties. It is, in fact, their atomic numbers (see page 10). Although the atomic number affects the mass, it is not the mass that is most important. It was the English physicist Henry Moseley (1887-1915) who discovered the significance of the atomic numbers. Once the elements were arranged by atomic number, the errors in Mendeleev's table were corrected.

Atoms and electricity

In most parts of the world today, electricity is taken for granted. At the flick of a switch, a light comes on. At the press of a button, a picture appears on the television. This is called current electricity, and is the most frequently used form of electricity. But what is electricity? It is energy in the form of flowing electrons, negatively charged subatomic particles.

Electricity is a flow of electrons.

Rub a balloon against your sweater for long enough, and it will stick to a wall or ceiling. Why? Because the rubbing creates a type of electricity which scientists call electrostatics, although it's more commonly known as static electricity.

Static electricity

Static electricity is the build up of an electrical charge. Once it has built up, it can stay for a long time. For example, if you stroke a cat on a dry day, the stroking sometimes builds up a charge on your hand and on the cat's fur. Suddenly the charge on the cat can be released, or discharged, through you. You feel a slight shock, and so does the cat.

When stroking the cat, you are rubbing electrons off the surface atoms of its fur and transferring them to your hand.

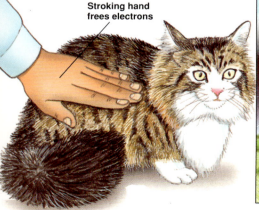
Stroking hand frees electrons

The fur and your hand are said to be poor conductors. Only when a large charge has built up do they conduct electricity. When the charge is high enough, it is able to spark between your hand and the cat. A good conductor is something, such as copper, which lets electricity flow through it easily. This is why copper is often used to make electrical wires. Silver is an even better conductor, but it is too expensive to use for most wiring.

There isn't a spark every time you stroke a cat because you need to stroke it for a long time before the charge builds. Also, the air has to be very dry. On days when the air is damp, the dampness can discharge the electrical charge before it builds up.

Did you know...?

The American inventor Benjamin Franklin (1706-1790) showed that a storm cloud was charged with static electricity. He did this by flying a kite in a thunderstorm, with a metal key tied to the string. The lightning hit the wet string, and the electricity flowed right down towards Franklin who was holding the other end. Some people who later copied the experiment were killed.

WARNING: Franklin's experiment could have killed him. Do not attempt to copy it.

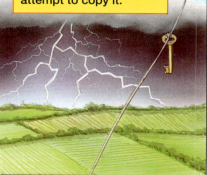

Bending water

A comb charged with static electricity will also bend water. You don't believe it? Turn on a tap and get a thin flow of water, then charge a comb by rubbing it on your hair. Now put the comb near to (but not quite touching) the flow of water. The water will bend towards the comb. If it doesn't, recharge the comb and try again.

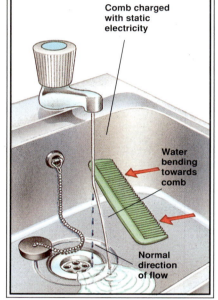

Comb charged with static electricity

Water bending towards comb

Normal direction of flow

Current electricity

It has already been said that electricity is the flow of electrons, but what makes the electrons in current electricity flow in the first place? The answer is electromotive force, often referred to as emf. This is the force produced by a battery or electricity generator. It is measured in units called volts (V), named after the Italian physicist Alessandro Volta (1745-1827). It was Volta who built the first battery, known as the Voltaic Pile.

Volta

Making your own battery

You can make your own version of the Voltaic Pile. This battery won't be strong enough to light up a light bulb, but you should be able to create a tiny spark to show the flow of electricity. It doesn't work every time but, if you keep trying, you should get a result. What's more, you can make this battery out of everyday objects. You will need three different types of 'disc': large copper coins and discs cut from aluminium foil and cardboard. Draw around the coins on the cardboard and aluminium foil, then cut them out. The discs must all be the same size. The more discs you use, the better the battery will be. You should use at least six of each.

Soak the cardboard discs in water with salt dissolved in it. Now pile up your discs in order: copper coin, soaked cardboard disc, aluminium foil, large copper coin, and so on...

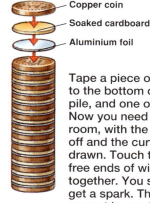

- Copper coin
- Soaked cardboard
- Aluminium foil

Tape a piece of wire to the bottom of the pile, and one on top. Now you need a dark room, with the lights off and the curtains drawn. Touch the two free ends of wire together. You should get a spark. The current is created by the metal coins and foil reacting with the salt water to create ions. Electromotive force (emf) is created, and the freed electrons flow along the wires as electricity.

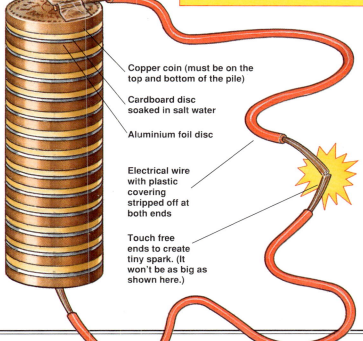

Coin

Foil

Coin

Cardboard

WARNING: It is safe to do this experiment because this is a very weak battery. Never experiment with electricity from wall sockets.

Copper coin (must be on the top and bottom of the pile)

Cardboard disc soaked in salt water

Aluminium foil disc

Electrical wire with plastic covering stripped off at both ends

Touch free ends to create tiny spark. (It won't be as big as shown here.)

Electrolysis

Electrolysis is the name given to chemical reactions which happen when an electric current is passed through a liquid containing ions. Different substances are formed as a result of these reactions. Any compound which conducts electricity when melted, or in a solution, is called an electrolyte. All ionic compounds (for example, common salt) are electrolytes.

Faraday's first law

The English scientist Michael Faraday (1791-1867) studied electrolysis and discovered some important things about it. These are called Faraday's laws of electrolysis. The first law states that the mass of the substance formed by a reaction in electrolysis is directly proportional to the quantity of electricity passed through an electrolyte.

Faraday

This diagram is an example of Faraday's first law of electrolysis.

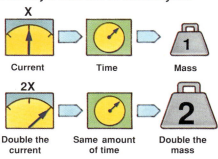

X		
Current	Time	Mass

2X		
Double the current	Same amount of time	Double the mass

This means that the amount of current used in the reaction has a particular affect on the mass of the newly-created substance. As you can see from the example above, the substance formed by double the amount of current (in the same amount of time) has double the mass of the first substance. Three times the current would have resulted in three times the mass.

Radiation

You've probably heard of radiation and how dangerous it can be. Radiation can cause harm to all living things, including humans, because it changes the atoms in living cells. But what is radiation, and how is it created?

Radiation is the result of the nuclei of some atoms being unstable. This happens when the protons and neutrons are not working well together. Unless an unstable object can somehow balance itself, it is likely to fall apart. For example, an unstable aircraft will crash, an unstable ship will capsize and, in the same way, the unstable nucleus of an atom can easily lose its balance.

Radiation can occur naturally or be created by scientists in the laboratory. It can be used both to help people and to kill them. Some of the different uses for radiation are discussed on pages 26-29.

Instability of the nucleus

The bigger the atom, the more likely it is to fall apart. The nucleus of an atom with an *atomic number** higher than 83 contains so many protons and neutrons that it becomes unstable, and begins to break up. During the break up, it becomes radioactive, giving off radiation. There are three main types of radiation. These are alpha particles, beta particles and gamma rays. They are named after the first three letters of the Greek alphabet. The letters are often used instead of the words. Elements in the periodic table (pages 20-21) are grouped by atomic number. Those elements at the bottom of the table have the highest atomic numbers. They are more likely to be unstable and therefore radioactive. Nevertheless, many of the smaller atoms also have radioactive *isotopes**.

α **Alpha**

β **Beta**

γ **Gamma**

Greek letters

The three nuclei below are all unstable. Each one is emitting a different type of radiation.

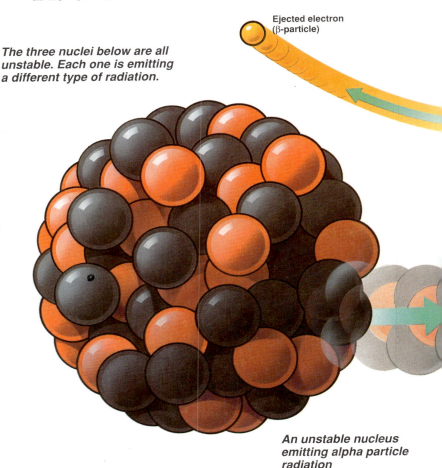

Ejected electron (β-particle)

An unstable nucleus emitting alpha particle radiation

Alpha particles

Unstable atoms try to balance themselves in different ways. Some atoms try to lose weight in an effort to become more stable. One way to think of it is as sailors on board an overloaded ship throwing the cargo into the sea in an effort to stay afloat. In the case of an overloaded atom, the nucleus sometimes throws out a cluster of two protons and two neutrons. This tiny cluster of four subatomic particles is called an alpha particle. Alpha particles are positively charged because they contain protons.

An alpha particle is identical to the nucleus of an atom of helium, a gas which is lighter than air. If alpha particles are collected, they can attract electrons from the atoms of nearby substances and create helium. There is a lot of helium in natural gas, which is widely used for cooking. Scientists believe that helium is created by the natural radioactivity in the earth.

Beta particles

Scientists now know that when a neutron decays it forms a number of particles including one proton and one electron. If a neutron of an unstable atom decays, the newly-formed proton remains in the nucleus but the electron is thrown out. This ejected electron is called a beta particle. It is a high energy electron, which moves very fast, travelling almost at the *speed of light**.

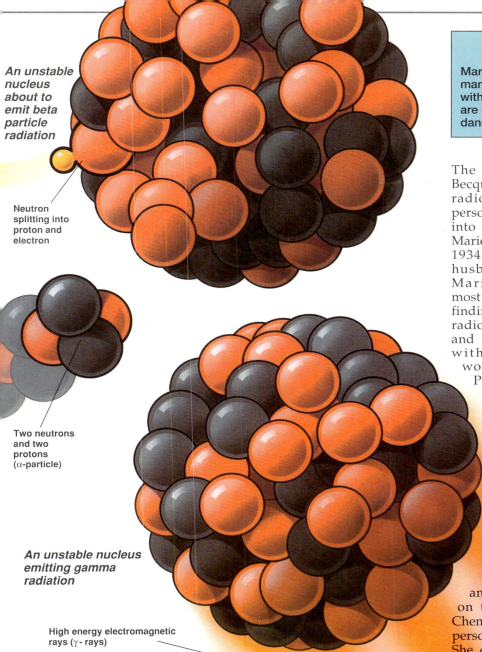

An unstable nucleus about to emit beta particle radiation

Neutron splitting into proton and electron

Two neutrons and two protons (α-particle)

An unstable nucleus emitting gamma radiation

High energy electromagnetic rays (γ- rays)

Gamma rays

When the nucleus of a radioactive atom has ejected either an alpha or beta particle, it often still contains too much energy to be stable. In an effort to balance itself, the atom can then give off some of this energy in the form of very high energy *electromagnetic** rays. These are called gamma rays.

Marie Curie

The French scientist Henri Becquerel (1852-1908) discovered radioactivity in 1896, but the person most famous for research into the subject is Marie Curie (1867-1934). With her husband Pierre, Marie devoted most of her life to finding out about radioactivity. She and Pierre, along with Becquerel, won the Nobel

Marie Curie

Prize for Physics in 1903. Marie discovered two important radioactive elements: radium, which she named after the word radioactivity, and polonium, which was named after Poland, her place of birth. Both were impurities taken from a type of uranium ore called pitchblende. Marie and Pierre found that radium was almost two million times more radioactive than uranium itself.

After Pierre was killed in an accident, Marie Curie went on to win the Nobel Prize for Chemistry in 1911. She was the first person to win two Nobel Prizes. She died of leukaemia, a type of cancer, probably as a result of many years of handling radioactive substances without protection.

Quiz

★ A uranium atom, containing 92 protons and 146 neutrons, ejects a particle to become a thorium atom, with 90 protons and 144 neutrons. Which did it eject, an α-particle or β-particle?

★ The thorium atom then gives off a β-particle. How many protons will be in the nucleus of the newly-formed atom: 88, 90 or 91?

Nuclear reactions

Radiation is now used in many different areas of life, including archaeology and medicine (see pages 28-29), but it is most commonly used in nuclear power stations to create electricity. The term 'nuclear power' comes from the word nucleus, because it is in the nuclei of certain atoms that radioactivity occurs. The process of creating radiation is called a nuclear reaction. There are two different types of nuclear reaction: nuclear fission and nuclear fusion.

Nuclear fission

If a particle (usually a neutron) is fired at the nucleus of a large atom, the atom will become unstable and break up. This process is called nuclear fission. It can be carried out in a machine called a particle accelerator, where neutrons are fired at nuclei. Fission can also occur naturally in large unstable nuclei.

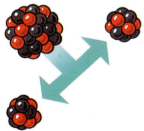

Nuclear fission is the breaking up of one nucleus into at least two parts.

Working with fission

Nuclear fission was discovered by two scientists, the German Otto Hahn (1879-1968) and Austrian-born Lise Meitner (1878-1968). They were working on experiments with radiation when Meitner, who was classified Jewish, had to flee Germany because of the Nazi persecution. She settled in Sweden, where Hahn sent her the results of his experiments. Meitner discussed these with her nephew, the physicist Otto Frisch (1904-1979). As a result of this collaboration, Hahn published a paper on the discovery of fission in 1938.

In 1942 the Italian-born scientist Enrico Fermi (1901-1954) built the world's first nuclear reactor in Chicago. It generated electricity using fission.

The atom bomb

During the Second World War, the scientist Albert Einstein feared that the Germans would use the fission process to make a new kind of bomb (referred to as the atom bomb or A-bomb). He urged the United States government to try to develop one first. As a result, the *Manhattan Project* was set up,

Einstein

and the first atom bombs were designed and built. A number of scientists, including Meitner, chose not to work on the project because they believed that such bombs would cause mass destruction.

Atom bombs were dropped in 1945 on the two Japanese cities of Hiroshima and Nagasaki. Though dropping the bombs may have brought an earlier end to the war and saved lives, Einstein was racked by guilt at the number of deaths that it caused.

Nuclear fusion

The other type of nuclear reaction is nuclear fusion. This happens when two nuclei are forced together to create a larger one. Nuclear fusion can only take place under huge pressure and high temperatures.

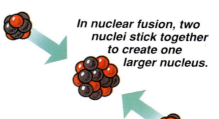

In nuclear fusion, two nuclei stick together to create one larger nucleus.

Nuclear fusion and fission both occur in another type of bomb called a hydrogen bomb (or fission-fusion bomb). This contains an atom bomb powered by fission which is surrounded by a substance containing hydrogen. The energy created by fission causes the hydrogen nuclei to stick together, or 'fuse', to create helium atoms.

Nuclear power stations

There are about 350 nuclear power stations in the world, supplying nearly 20% of the world's electricity.

The heart of a nuclear power station is its core, where the actual reactions take place. Here there is a fourth type of radiation called neutron radiation. Radioactive materials are used as fuel in the core. This fuel creates nuclear energy which is used to create steam. The steam then turns a turbine which generates the electricity.

Different types of nuclear power stations use different types of nuclear reactors. The most common is the pressurized water reactor, sometimes referred to as a PWR. Another type is the fast-breeder reactor (FBR), which 'breeds' (or produces) additional fuel during nuclear reactions. Both types are fission reactors.

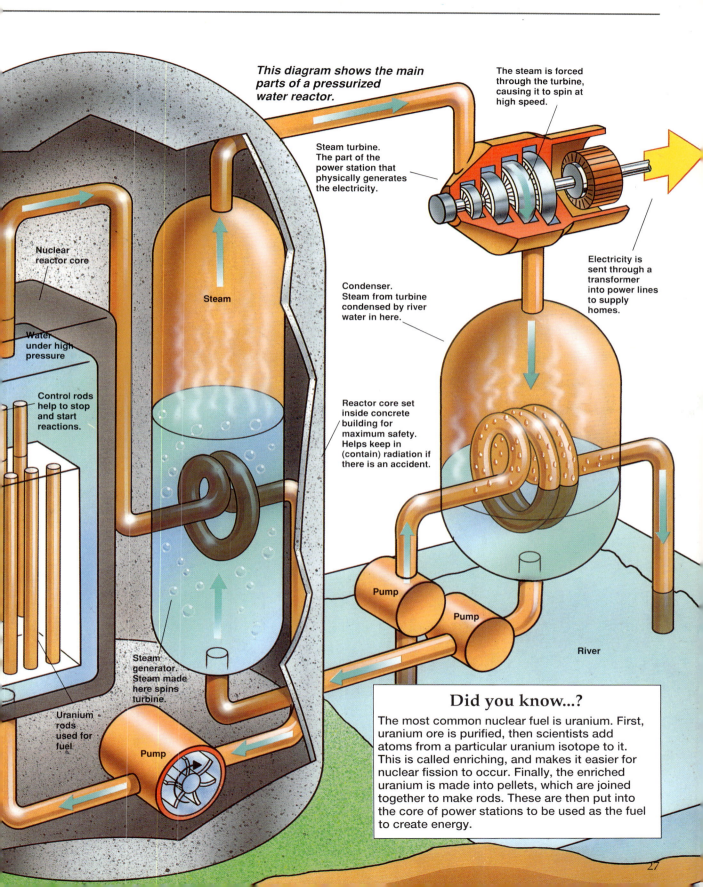

This diagram shows the main parts of a pressurized water reactor.

The steam is forced through the turbine, causing it to spin at high speed.

Steam turbine. The part of the power station that physically generates the electricity.

Electricity is sent through a transformer into power lines to supply homes.

Nuclear reactor core

Steam

Water under high pressure

Control rods help to stop and start reactions.

Condenser. Steam from turbine condensed by river water in here.

Reactor core set inside concrete building for maximum safety. Helps keep in (contain) radiation if there is an accident.

Steam generator. Steam made here spins turbine.

Uranium rods used for fuel

Pump

Pump

Pump

River

Did you know...?

The most common nuclear fuel is uranium. First, uranium ore is purified, then scientists add atoms from a particular uranium isotope to it. This is called enriching, and makes it easier for nuclear fission to occur. Finally, the enriched uranium is made into pellets, which are joined together to make rods. These are then put into the core of power stations to be used as the fuel to create energy.

Working with the atom

Today radiation is used for many things, besides generating power and creating nuclear weapons. Though very dangerous in uncontrolled doses, small amounts can be used to help people. The first practical use was for the treatment of certain types of cancer.

Treating cancer

Cancer is caused by living cells which grow in a disorderly way and spread through the body, often causing tumours. Alpha and beta particles have an electric charge which means that they can attract and repel the subatomic particles in living cells. Carefully measured amounts of radiation can be used to alter the subatomic particles in cancer cells, and make them harmless. This must be done without damaging the healthy cells, because exposure to too much radiation can itself cause cancer. The radioactive substance most commonly used for this is cobalt-60.

This cancer patient is receiving radiation treatment.

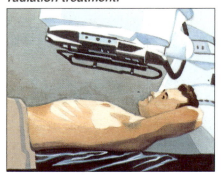

Tracers

In hospitals radiation is also used for following, or 'tracing', a substance through a patient's bloodstream. For example, a doctor can find out how a patient's body reacts to sugar by attaching some carbon-14 to some molecules of sugar, which the patient then eats. The path of the sugar can then be followed through the patient's body by using a machine called a Geiger counter. The Geiger counter, invented in 1908 by Hans Geiger (1882-1945) and Ernest Rutherford, is a hand-held machine used to detect radiation. When radiation is present, the machine gives off a series of clicking noises. The level of radiation is counted and shown on a dial.

A modern Geiger counter

PET

One of the latest uses for tracers is in experiments on the brain. This procedure is called positron-emission tomography (PET for short). A radioisotope (a radioactive *isotope**) is attached, or 'tagged', to some water which is then taken up by the brain cells. The part of the brain which does the most work during an activity uses the most water. So by finding the part with the highest radioactive count, scientists can prove which part is used for different mental activities. For example, it can be shown that you remember a painting with a different part of the brain from the part you use to remember a song.

Carbon dating

All plants, animals and people contain a small amount of the radioisotope carbon-14. In a living thing the amount remains the same because it is always being used and then replaced (in the form of food and carbon dioxide). When a living thing dies, however, the amount of carbon-14 gets less and less, and is not replaced. Items from archaeological sites, including bones and objects made from materials such as wood and natural fibres, can be dated by measuring the amount of carbon-14 in them. This is because carbon-14's rate of decay is known.

This is part of the Dead Sea Scrolls. By using carbon dating, they were calculated to be over 2000 years old.

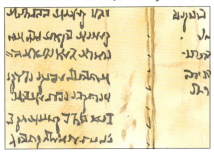

Half life

When a radioisotope gives off radiation, it begins to decay. This means that it is losing its radioactivity. The rate of decay is measured by its half life, the term used for the time it takes for half of the atoms to decay. For example, the radioisotope thorium has a half life of 24 days. If a substance contained 12 million thorium atoms, after 24 days there would be six million radioactive atoms left. After another 24 days there would be three million. This can be shown on a graph:

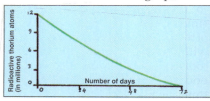

Irradiation

Most types of food, including meat, fruit and vegetables, can be made to stay 'fresh' longer by being given a dose of gamma rays. This process is called food irradiation.

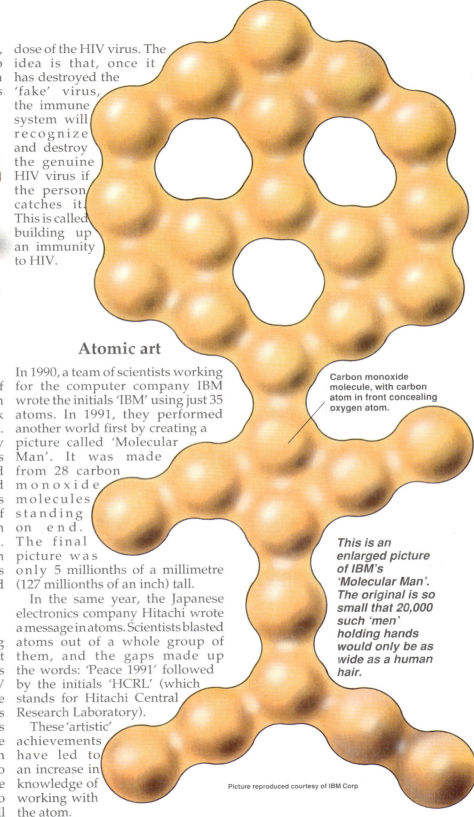

After two weeks, an untreated fresh strawberry will have gone mouldy.

A two-week-old irradiated strawberry will look and taste as fresh as ever.

Not everyone approves of irradiating food, for two main reasons. First, some people think that it is misleading for shoppers. They will be buying what they believe to be fresh food, when it is really much older. This can be solved by clearly labelling the food 'irradiated'. The second worry is more serious. Nobody knows if there will be any harmful long-term effects from eating irradiated food. No one appears to have been harmed by it, but no one has yet eaten a lifelong diet of food treated in this way.

Fighting disease

British scientists have been creating new molecules in an effort to fight the killer disease AIDS. Scientists believe that a virus called the HIV virus can lead to AIDS. They have been working with yeast molecules to produce man-made proteins similar to those found on the outside of the HIV virus. By injecting a person with these proteins, it is hoped to fool the human immune system (the body's self-defence system) into thinking that it has received a small dose of the HIV virus. The idea is that, once it has destroyed the 'fake' virus, the immune system will recognize and destroy the genuine HIV virus if the person catches it. This is called building up an immunity to HIV.

Atomic art

In 1990, a team of scientists working for the computer company IBM wrote the initials 'IBM' using just 35 atoms. In 1991, they performed another world first by creating a picture called 'Molecular Man'. It was made from 28 carbon monoxide molecules standing on end. The final picture was only 5 millionths of a millimetre (127 millionths of an inch) tall.

In the same year, the Japanese electronics company Hitachi wrote a message in atoms. Scientists blasted atoms out of a whole group of them, and the gaps made up the words: 'Peace 1991' followed by the initials 'HCRL' (which stands for Hitachi Central Research Laboratory).

These 'artistic' achievements have led to an increase in knowledge of working with the atom.

Carbon monoxide molecule, with carbon atom in front concealing oxygen atom.

This is an enlarged picture of IBM's 'Molecular Man'. The original is so small that 20,000 such 'men' holding hands would only be as wide as a human hair.

Picture reproduced courtesy of IBM Corp

The make-up of the universe

Scientists are the first to admit that there is still a great deal to be learned about the atoms and subatomic particles that make up our universe. The more discoveries they make, the more they realize how little is really known.

The quantum theory

In 1900 the German physicist Max Planck (1858-1947) suggested that *gamma rays** were not waves but were composed of tiny particles, or 'quanta', of energy. Combined with Einstein's ideas published five years later, this led to what became known as the quantum theory. As a result, quantum mechanics was born. This is based on the belief that *matter** can behave as either waves or particles. Many scientists see these revolutionary ideas as the turning point from classical to modern physics.

Max Planck

Categories of particles

Protons, neutrons and electrons are not the only subatomic particles. Scientists now know that there are many more. A number of these particles have actually been proved to exist, but others have only been calculated to exist as a way of explaining certain *phenomena**.

At present, particles are divided into three categories: elementary particles, composite particles and bosons. Elementary particles are themselves divided into two categories: leptons and quarks.

Leptons

Like all elementary particles, those in the lepton category are thought to have no internal structure. They are believed to consist of themselves and nothing else. These particles include the electron.

The electron is a fine example of a particle which sometimes behaves like a wave. It is thought to look like a blur moving in the shape of a cloud in the cloud model (see page 8). Some scientists think that the movement of an electron can be expressed as a Mobius strip. This is like a hoop with a twist in it, giving it a one-sided continuous surface.

This shows an electron moving through a shape like a Mobius strip.

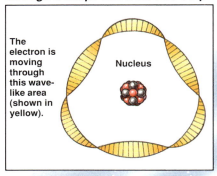

The electron is moving through this wave-like area (shown in yellow).

Nucleus

There are three other leptons: the muon, the tau and the neutrino. When a neutron breaks down into a proton and an electron, a neutrino is sometimes released. It is so small that it could cross our galaxy 12,000 times and only have a 50% chance of meeting and reacting with anything at all. There are thought to be three types of neutrino.

Quarks

Quarks are particles which are thought to be part of the make-up of all other particles in the universe, apart from leptons. The theory that such particles might exist was first put forward in 1964. They were named 'quarks' by the American physicist Murray Gell-Mann (1929-   ), one of two scientists who came up with the theory independently. There are believed to be six types of quark. They have been named Up, Down, Strange, Charm, Bottom and Top. It has now been proved that quarks must have a kind of charge that no one knew existed (rather than an electrical or magnetic charge, for example). This charge has been called 'colour', and comes in three different forms called 'shades'.

Antimatter

Scientists now suggest that there is such a thing as antimatter, and that it is made from things called antiparticles. Every elementary particle is thought to have a corresponding antiparticle. For example, a neutrino would have an antineutrino, and a quark would have an antiquark. Antiparticles are said to have the same mass as their corresponding particles, but totally opposite levels of energy. To explain this idea thoroughly would take up a book in itself.

Composite particles

As their name suggests, composite particles are composed (or made up) of various elementary particles combined. Composite particles include: the proton, the neutron and the pion. The pion was discovered in 1947, twelve years after it was first suggested that it might exist. It is believed to be made up of one quark and one antiquark.

Bosons

The term 'particle' usually applies to a small piece of matter. One difference between matter and energy is that, unlike energy, matter is said to have mass. Bosons are complicated in this sense because they are a category of particles, but some bosons are packets of energy waves. The most famous of these is the photon. Einstein said that it was the photon that transported the electrical and magnetic forces between charged particles.

When radioactive atoms give off energy, they give off light. And light is made of waves. The light moves forward in tiny ripples but, unlike water waves, light waves are trapped inside 'packets'. A photon is a packet of light waves. One way to imagine one is as a snake wriggling in a sack. The snake is the wave and the sack is the packet around it.

Light waves

Light comes in different colours. Light of the same colour is made of photons vibrating at the same rate, or frequency. Although all light travels at the same speed, different coloured light waves have different levels of energy. They vibrate at different rates as they cover the same distance.

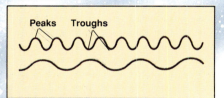

Peaks   Troughs

These are two waves of different coloured light. The top one has more energy. This means that it has a higher frequency and more peaks and troughs than the other.

Breaking down particles

There is a machine that scientists use to break down matter into simpler forms. It is called a particle accelerator. Some of these machines are miles long. Inside the accelerator, particles can be fired at each other at great speed. Sometimes a particular particle is used as a target and is bombarded by other particles. Sometimes particles are forced to collide head-on. These collisions, which can break up many of the particles involved, have lead to many new and exciting discoveries. Research into the make-up of the universe goes on.

Glossary

Here is a list explaining some of the more common or complicated words and phrases which appear in this book. When a word appears in *italics*, it has its own entry in the list.

Allotropes. Two or more different physical forms of the same *element*. For example, diamond and graphite are both allotropes of carbon. See pages 12-13.

Alpha particle (α-particle). Two *protons* and two *neutrons* emitted from the *nucleus* of a *radioactive atom*. See pages 24-25.

Anion. A negatively charged *ion*.

Atom. The smallest particle of an *element* that retains the *chemical properties* of that element.

Atomic number. The number of protons in the nucleus of an atom. See page 10.

Beta particle (β-particle). A fast moving *electron* emitted from the *nucleus* of a *radioactive atom*. It is produced when a *neutron* breaks down to form a *proton* and an *electron*. See pages 24-25.

Bond. See *covalent bond* and *ionic bond*.

Cathode ray tube. A vacuum tube containing a fluorescent screen, on which *electrons* can be focused to give a visible spot of light. A more complex form of this tube is used in televisions.

Cation. A positively charged *ion*.

Chemical properties. Properties which cause substances to behave in specific ways during a *chemical reaction*.

Chemical reaction. Any change which alters the *chemical properties* of a substance, or forms a new substance or substances.

Conductor. A substance through which electric current or heat can flow.

Covalent bond. A covalent bond is formed when two *atoms* share a pair of *electrons*, so are linked together. See pages 14-15.

Crystal. A solid with a regular geometric shape, made from regular arrangements of *atoms*, *ions* or *molecules*. A crystal's surfaces are flat and its edges are straight. See pages 18-19.

Electromagnetic radiation. Radiation which creates an electric and a magnetic field at right angles to each other. *Gamma rays* are electromagnetic.

Electron. *Subatomic particle* which moves outside the *nucleus* of an *atom*. An electron's mass is only 1/1840th of that of a *proton*. It has a negative electrical charge equal and opposite to that of a proton.

Element. A substance which cannot be split into even simpler substances by a *chemical reaction*. See pages 8-9.

Gamma ray (γ-ray). A high energy *electromagnetic* ray emitted from the *nucleus* of a *radioactive atom*. See pages 24-25.

Insulator. A bad *conductor* of electricity or heat.

Ionic bond. When a *cation* is attracted to an *anion*, an ionic bond is formed.

Ion. Electrically charged particle, formed when an atom gains or loses one or more electrons. An Ion is either an *anion* or a *cation*.

Isotopes. *Atoms* which belong to the same *element* but have a different number of *neutrons* in their *nuclei*. See page 10.

Mass. A measurement of the amount of matter in a substance. Unlike weight, mass is not affected by gravity. It always remains the same.

Mass number. The number of *protons* and *neutrons* in the *nucleus* of an *atom*. See page 10.

Matter. A substance that occupies space and has *mass*.

Molecule. The smallest particle of an *element* or compound that usually exists on its own and keep the *properties* of that element.

Neutron. A *subatomic particle* in the *nucleus* of an *atom*. In unstable atoms, neutrons can break up and cause *beta particle* radiation.

Nucleus (plural: **nuclei**). The cluster of *protons* and *neutrons* in the middle of an *atom*.

Phenomena. Occurrences and facts.

Physical properties. All the properties of a substance, except for those which affect its behaviour in *chemical reactions*. Physical properties include smell, taste, colour and *mass*.

Proton. A posatively charged *subatomic particle* in the *nucleus* of an *atom*.

PVC. The initials and common name for poly vinyl chloride, a type of plastic. See page 18.

Radioactive. Giving off radiation.

Radioisotope. A *radioactive isotope*.

Reactive/Reactivity. The reactivity of an *element* depends on its ability to gain or lose the *electrons* it needs to *bond*. The more reactive an element, the more easily it bonds

Speed of light. 300,000km per second/186,000 miles per second.

Structure. The arrangement of *atoms* in a *molecule* or compound.

Subatomic particle. Any particle smaller than an atom. These include the *proton*, *neutron*, *electron* and those listed on pages 30-31.

Unstable. When a *nucleus* has a high *mass number* or an imbalance of *protons* and *neutrons*, it is said to be unstable. Unstable nuclei give off radiation.

Index

Quiz answers

Page 7
★ The electron
★ Neither. They have the same amount of electrical charge.
★ 3680

Page 9
★ Two shells
★ Two electrons

Page 13
★ In diamond each atom is linked to 4 other atoms, rather than 3. Graphite's structure is also weaker because it is made up of a series of plates which can easily slide over each other.
★ Noble metals
★ Metals

Page 20
★ The approximate RAM of sodium is 23.0. This is the average RAM of lithium and potassium.

Page 25
★ α-particle.
★ 91 protons